I Shall Fulfil My Destiny

Pastor Seyi Ogunorunyinka

Published by Promised Land ministries publication

Plot 17 Aminu Jinadu close, Off Jimoh Odutola Street, off Eric Moore Road, Surulere Lagos Nigeria.

All scriptures are quoted from the New International Version.

Cover design and electronic publishing by Leverage Publishing – 09021287290, leveragepublishing21@gmail.com

FOREWORD

Prayer is the key to opening the door of heaven. When we pray, we invite God into our situation. Prayer is the only way to communicate with God. It is the staff of the Christian pilgrim to walk with God. Little wonders, Apostle Paul enjoined us to pray without ceasing (I Thess. 5:17).

As born again Christians, our prayers are powerful. It touches the throne of mercy, the bible says that the prayer of a righteous man avails much. Prayer is an expression of the desired expectation, and we know that the expectation of the righteous will be fulfilled. However, in spiritual welfare, the bible says we wrestle not against flesh and blood but against principalities, against powers against the rulers of darkness of this world, against spiritual wickedness in high places (Ephesians 6:10). Therefore you must take on the whole armour of God which is not complete without prayer and fasting to move the mountains in our lives as our Lord Jesus Christ says: "However, this kind does not go without prayer and fasting" (Matthew 7:21).

I believe that if you join us in this period of prayer and fasting and you diligently follow the prayer points, the almighty God will release His glory upon your life and everything the enemy thought was impossible for you will become possible in the mighty name of Jesus. Amen.

Pastor Seyi Ogunorunyinka

Contents

Devotional Songs

DEVOTIONAL SONGS

Spirit divine attend our prayers

1. Spirit divine, attend our prayers
And make this house thy home
Descend with all thy gracious powers
O come, great spirit, come

2. Come as the light, to us reveal
Our emptiness and woe
And lead us in those paths of life
Where all the righteous go

3. Come as the fire, and purge our hearts
Like sacrificial flame
Let our whole soul an offering be
To our redeemer's name

4. Come as the dew, and sweetly bless
This consecrated hour
May barrenness rejoice to own
Thy fertilizing power

5. Come as the dove, and spread thy wings
The wings of peaceful love
And let thy church on earth become
Blest as the church above

6. Come as the wind, with rushing sound

And Pentecostal grace
That all of woman born may see
The glory of thy home

7. Spirit divine, attend our prayers
Make a lost world thy home
Descend with all thy gracious powers
O come, great spirit, come. Amen

Take my life, and let it be

1. Take my life, and let it be,
Consecrated Lord, to thee
Take my moments and my days
Let them flow in ceaseless praise

2. Take my hands, and let them move
At the impulse of thy love
Take my feet and let them be
Swift and beautiful for thee

3. Take my voice, and let me sing
Always, only for my king
Take my lips, and let them be
Filled with messages from thee

4. Take my silver and my gold
Not a mite would I withhold
Take my intellect, and use
Every power as thou shalt choose

5. Take my will, and make it thine
It shall be no longer mine
Take my heart it is thine own
It shall be thy royal throne

6. Take my love, my Lord, I pour
At thy feet its treasure store
Take myself, and I will be
Ever, only all for thee

ROCK OF AGES CLEFT FOR ME

1. Rock of Ages, cleft for me
Let me hide myself in thee
Let the water and the blood
From thy riven side which flowed,
Be of sin the double cure
Cleanse me from its guilt and power

2. Not the labours of my hands
Can fulfil thy laws demands
Could my zeal no respite know
Could my tears for ever flow
All of sin could not atone
Thou must save, and thou alone

3. Nothing in my hand I bring
Simply to thy cross I cling
Naked, come to thee for dress
Helpless, look to thee for grace
Foul, I to the fountain fly
Wash me saviour or I die

4. While I draw this fleeting breath
When my eyelids close in death
When I soar to worlds unknown
See thee on thy judgement throne
Rock of ages, cleft for me
Let me hide myself in thee. Amen.

THINE FOREVER GOD OF LOVE

1. Thine forever! God of love,
Hear us from thy throne above
Thine forever may we be
Here and in eternity

2. Thine forever! Lord of life,
Shield us through our earthly strife
Thou the life, the truth, the way
Guide us to the realms of day

3. Thine forever! O how blest
They who find in thee their rest
Saviour, guardian, heavenly friend
O defend us to the end

4. Thine forever! Shepherd keep
These thy frail and trembling sheep,
Safe alone beneath thy care
Let us all thy goodness share

5. Thine forever! Thou our guide
All our wants by thee supplied,
All our sins by thee forgiven
Lead us, Lord, from earth to heaven. Amen

PRAYERS FOR CHURCHES

To be done every Sunday

1. Lord, establish your church on earth, in the name of Jesus.

2. Your word says in **Matthew 16:18** that "I will build my church, and the gates of hades shall not overcome it." O Lord, build Your church and do not allow the gate of hell to prevail against it, in the name of Jesus.

3. You are the God of impossibilities, is there anything too difficult for You to do? O Lord, deposit Your awesome power in our churches, in the name of Jesus.

4. O Lord, close down any church that You have not established, in the name of Jesus.

5. O Lord, anoint our Pastors and ministers with fire and power from above, in the name of Jesus.

6. O Lord, draw men unto yourself in our churches, in the name of Jesus.

7. We destroy every power of Satan preventing people from seeing the light of the gospel of Jesus Christ, in the name of Jesus.

8. Father, You do not desire the death of sinners but You want them to repent and be saved. O Lord, let the salvation message touch the lives of sinners, in the name of Jesus.

9. Let the Holy Ghost fire and the blood of Jesus be a shield and cover for every servant of God against any satanic attack, in the name of Jesus.

10. O Lord, give your servants the courage and boldness to speak your word without fear or favour, in the name of Jesus.

11. **2 Chronicles 7:14.** Let your churches become solution grounds for all manner of problems in the name of Jesus.

12. O Lord, remove and destroy everything that will bring shame and reproach to Your name, in the name of Jesus.

13. O Lord, expose and disgrace every satanic agent hiding in the church in the name of Jesus.

14. O Lord expose and disgrace every power devouring peoples blessing and testimonies in the church, in the name of Jesus.

15. O Lord, paralyse every power attacking Christian marriages, in the name of Jesus.

16. O Lord, expose and disgrace any satanic agent practising Pentecostal witchcraft in Your churches, in the name of Jesus.

17. O Lord, deposit Your wealth in the hands of Christians so that they can invest in the things of God in the name of Jesus.

18. O Lord, let the wealth of the gentiles be transferred to Christians, in the name of Jesus.

19. O Lord, make Your servants to focus on You for the funding of the church and not on any man, in the name of Jesus.

20. O Lord, deposit Your love in all Your churches, in the name of Jesus.

21. We come against the plan of Satan to *"water down"* the Word of God in the guise of attracting people to our churches, in the name of Jesus. Amen.

PRAYER FOR THE NATION

TO BE DONE ON FRIDAYS

1. O Lord, let Your plans and purposes for Nigeria come to pass, whether the enemy likes it or not, in the name of Jesus.

2. O Lord, give us good and committed leaders in this country that will run the country with Your fear in their hearts, in the name of Jesus.

3. O Lord, let the plans of Satan to cause war and confusion in Nigeria fail woefully, in the name of Jesus.

4. We come against every spirit of division and tribalism in this country, in the name of Jesus.

5. O Lord, give us the power in this country to promote things that will unite us as a people and not things that will emphasise our differences, in the name of Jesus.

6. O Lord, forgive us for all the blood of innocent people that have been wasted in this country, in the name of Jesus.

7. O Lord, let there be a spiritual revival in this country, in the name of Jesus.

8. Every power that is against the continued existence of this country Nigeria as one, be destroyed by fire, in the name of Jesus.

9. Every spirit of wastage and mismanagement operating in Nigeria die, in the name of Jesus.

10. Every curse and covenant pronounced on this country Nigeria which has been limiting the growth and development of this country, break, in the name of Jesus.

11. Every local god, goddess, principality and powers, holding Nigeria in bondage, lose your hold and die, in the name of Jesus.

12. Every evil door that we have opened for the enemy to attack us in this country, be closed forever with the blood of Jesus.

13. Let the damage that has been done to the image of this country, be repaired by the blood of Jesus.

14. O Lord, give us the wisdom and understanding that will make this country great, in the name of Jesus.

15. O Lord, expose and disgrace all satanic agents who have succeeded in installing themselves in positions of authority in this country, in the name of Jesus.

16. We reject every spirit of backwardness in this nation, in the name of Jesus.

17. O Lord, move this country forward by fire, in the name of Jesus.

18. O Lord let this country Nigeria be able to take its rightful place in the comity of nations, in the name of Jesus.

19. O Lord, we reject every spirit of poverty in this country, in the name of Jesus.

20. O Lord, install Your agenda for this country, in the name of Jesus.

21. O Lord, let the lost glory of Nigeria be restored, in the name of Jesus.

SECTION 1

My Dream Shall Not Die

Day 1

Confession: Genesis 42:6 "*Now Joseph was governor over the land, and it was he who sold to all the people of the land. And Joseph's brothers came and bowed down to him with their faces to the earth.*"

Text: Genesis 28:15, 1 kings 3:1-15; 11:1-13

Song: Spirit divine attend our prayers

Praise worship: (minimum of 10 minutes)

Prayer of praise and thanksgiving: (minimum of 10 minutes)

PRAYER POINTS

1. O Lord, give me a dream that will reveal my destiny to me, in the name of Jesus
2. O Lord, make me the head and not the tail, in the name of Jesus
3. My sheaves shall arise and stand while those of others shall gather around mine and bow down, in the name of Jesus
4. O Lord, restrain me from speaking the secrets of my life to my enemies, in the name of Jesus
5. Anything in my life that will delay the fulfilment of my dreams, depart, in the name of Jesus
6. O Lord, remove pride from my life, in the name of Jesus
7. Every spirit of jealousy working against the realization of my dream die, in the name of Jesus
8. No matter how impossible and unrealistic my divine dream is, it shall come to pass, in the name of Jesus
9. Every power attempting to kill my dream, you have failed, in the name of Jesus

10. O Lord behold the enemies are trying to kill the dream that you gave me, do something in the name of Jesus

11. No evil counsel shall stand against the manifestation of my dream, in the name of Jesus

12. Let my enemies make mistakes that will advance my course, in the name of Jesus

13. O Lord, give me the grace to hold on to my divine dream, in the name of Jesus

14. O Lord give me the power to live a holy life, in the name of Jesus

DAY 2

Confession: Genesis 42:6
Text: Genesis 37: 1-36
Song: Spirit divine attend our prayers
Praise worship: (minimum of 10 minutes)
Prayer of praise and thanksgiving: (minimum of 10 minutes)

PRAYER POINTS

1. I will not die before my time, in the name of Jesus
2. What God has purposed to use to elevate me shall not lead to my death, in the name of Jesus
3. Let my life begin to reject evil, in the name of Jesus
4. In whatever situation I find myself the presence of God shall never depart from my life in the name of Jesus
5. I will not give up on my God-given dream, in the name of Jesus
6. Every agent of the devil sent to derail me from fulfilling my destiny, fail woefully in the name of Jesus
7. O Lord, let me never shift my focus from you, in the name of Jesus
8. Every spirit of covetousness, die, in the name of Jesus
9. I refuse to give my enemy the ammunition with which to attack my dreams, in the name of Jesus
10. O Lord, let me cooperate with you to fulfil my destiny, in the name of Jesus
11. I am moving forward by fire whether the enemy likes it or not in the name of Jesus

12. O Lord, give me wisdom that will assist me in the realisation of my dreams and vision, in the name of Jesus

13. I reject partial victory and partial success, in the name of Jesus

14. O Lord, show me Kindness and grant me favour, in the eyes of everyone I come in contact with in the name of Jesus

DAY 3

Confession: Genesis 42:6
Text: Genesis 37: 1-23
Song: Spirit divine attend our prayers
Praise worship: (minimum of 10 minutes)
Prayer of praise and thanksgiving: (minimum of 10 minutes)

PRAYER POINTS

1. In everything I do I claim the portion of the head and not the tail, in the name of Jesus
2. O Lord, give me success in all that I do, in the name of Jesus
3. O Lord, set machinery in motion to make my dream come true, in the name of Jesus
4. O Lord, in all that I do let me always give glory to you, in the name of Jesus
5. I refuse to take the glory that rightly belongs to God in the name of Jesus
6. O Lord, give me the wisdom that no one can contend with, in the name of Jesus
7. O Lord, begin to manifest your unlimited glory in my life, in the name of Jesus
8. In all that I do, I refuse to put my trust in man, in the name of Jesus
9. O Lord, remember how unjustly I have been treated and fight for me, in the name of Jesus
10. O Lord, open up your book of remembrance and come to my rescue, in the name of Jesus

11. O Lord, do not give my divine helpers any rest until they carry out your instructions concerning my life

12. All those who have proposed to help me, O Lord let them begin to remember the promises they made to me in the name of Jesus

13. O Lord, let me begin to sow seeds that would result in the bountiful harvest of my dreams, in the name of Jesus

14. I shall rise above my current problems, in the name of Jesus

Day 4

Confession: Genesis 42:6
Text: Genesis 41: 1-43
Song: Spirit divine attend our prayers
Praise worship: (minimum of 10 minutes)
Prayer of praise and thanksgiving: (minimum of 10 minutes)

PRAYER POINTS

1. I shall cooperate with God for the full realisation of my dreams, in the name of Jesus
2. The blessings of God shall not destroy me in the name of Jesus
3. The Lord that has begun a new thing in my life shall perfect it, in the name of Jesus
4. The days of my suffering, depression, frustration are numbered, in the name of Jesus
5. I reject lame blessings, in the name of Jesus
6. My life, begin to witness the full-scale blessings of God, in the name of Jesus
7. O Lord, make me the obvious choice of your blessings, in the name of Jesus
8. Where others have failed, I will succeed, in the name of Jesus
9. O Lord, set me up for blessings, in the name of Jesus
10. I shall be at the right place at the right time, in the name of Jesus
11. People that I know and do not know shall seek me out to bless me, in the name of Jesus

12. O Lord, grant me divine wisdom and knowledge to solve my deeply rooted problems, in the name of Jesus

13. My God shall not forsake me with my problems, he shall send help to me at the appropriate time, in the name of Jesus

14. The heart of the king is in your hands, O Lord connect me to highly placed individuals, in the name of Jesus

DAY 5

Confession: Genesis 42:6
Text: Genesis 42: 1-9
Song: Spirit divine attend our prayers
Praise worship: (minimum of 10 minutes)
Prayer of praise and thanksgiving: (minimum of 10 minutes)

PRAYER POINTS

1. O Lord, let the gifts you have given to me lead me to my elevation, in the name of Jesus
2. My dreams shall defile all odds and it shall come to pass, in the name of Jesus
3. Every evil counsel concerning my destiny, be nullified by the blood of Jesus
4. I move up from prison to palace, in the name of Jesus
5. Every power pursuing me to destroy the plan of God for my life, fail woefully, in the name of Jesus
6. The plan of God for my life shall not die, in the name of Jesus
7. Let my dreams begin to come from the most unexpected quarters, in the name of Jesus
8. Let the God of suddenly begin to manifest himself in my life, in the name of Jesus
9. The power to make the impossible possible fall upon my life now, in the name of Jesus
10. Let a sudden turnaround take place in my life for the best, in the name of Jesus

11. I shall not speak about my divine dream prematurely, in the name of Jesus

12. My mouth shall not invite problems into my life, in the name of Jesus

13. Every spirit of envy and jealously be powerless over me, in the name of Jesus

14. My promotion shall be announced without further delay, in the name of Jesus

DAY 6

Confession: Genesis 42:6
Text: Genesis 28: 10-22
Song: Spirit divine attend our prayers
Praise worship: (minimum of 10 minutes)
Prayer of praise and thanksgiving: (minimum of 10 minutes)

PRAYER POINTS

1. My delayed promotion come forth now, in the name of Jesus
2. Let a divine connection be made between me and those who will help me to achieve my dream, in the name of Jesus
3. Where the enemy thinks I will not get to, I will get there in the name of Jesus
4. Every garment of poverty be roasted,
5. O Lord, set me up for promotion in the name of Jesus
6. O Lord, put words into my mouth which will herald my promotion in the name of Jesus
7. O Lord baptise me with favour in your presence and before kings and princes, in the name of Jesus
8. You the garment of poverty and lack I shall see you no more, in the name of Jesus
9. Foreigner shall serve me, in the name of Jesus
10. O Lord, give me divine wisdom to actualize my dream, in the name of Jesus
11. My enemies shall witness my blessings, in the name of Jesus

12. My enemies shall have no other choice than to bow down to me, in the name of Jesus

13. O Lord, turn my situation around so much that my enemies will not be able to recognize me, in the name of Jesus

14. O Lord, make me a wealth distribution centre, in the name of Jesus

Day 7

Confession: Genesis 42:6
Text: 1 Kings 10: 1-29
Song: Spirit divine attend our prayers
Praise worship: (minimum of 10 minutes)
Prayer of praise and thanksgiving: (minimum of 10 minutes)

PRAYER POINTS

1. I reject every spirit of revenge, in the name of Jesus
2. I reject every spirit of un-forgiveness, in the name of Jesus
3. O Lord put me in a position to influence the lives of members of my family positively, in the name of Jesus
4. O Lord, give me the power to see beyond the evil done by people unto me in the name of Jesus
5. O Lord, fit me into your divine will for my life, in the name of Jesus
6. Let news about my life bring joy and rejoicing to others, in the name of Jesus
7. Let my life begin to minister solutions to people's problems, in the name of Jesus
8. Those who have given up on me will have no other choice than to reckon with me, in the name of Jesus
9. On account of me, members of my family will be blessed, in the name of Jesus
10. All that he enemy has stolen from me, I will recover them with interest, in the name of Jesus

11. My hands shall be stronger than the hands of my enemies, in the name of Jesus

12. O Lord, make me a force to reckon with among my contemporaries, in the name of Jesus

13. O Lord give me the spirit of humility, in the name of Jesus

14. In all that I do, I shall always allow the fear of God to determine my action, in the name of Jesus

Day 8

Confession: Genesis 42:6
Text: 1 Kings 3: 16–28; Genesis 50: 15–21
Song: Spirit divine attend our prayers
Praise worship: (minimum of 10 minutes)
Prayer of praise and thanksgiving: (minimum of 10 minutes)

PRAYER POINTS

1. I shall not put myself in the position of God and begin to judge others, in the name of Jesus
2. The evil powers of my father's house shall have no control over my life, in the name of Jesus
3. Every evil intended against me by my enemies, be converted to blessings, in the name of Jesus
4. O Lord, let me make myself available for your use at all times, in the name of Jesus
5. Just as you were with Joseph and he prospered in all that he did, let your presence never depart from me, in the name of Jesus
6. O Lord give me divine opportunity to actualize my dreams, in the name of Jesus
7. O Lord, give me the spirit of boldness to seize the divine opportunities that you have presented before me, in the name of Jesus
8. O Lord, do not leave me until you have fulfilled your promise to me, in the name of Jesus

9. I shall cooperate with God to actualize my dreams, in the name of Jesus

10. My dream shall not be eaten up by the enemy, in the name of Jesus

11. O Lord, reveal to me the steps that I need to take to prosper, in the name of Jesus

12. The God that makes the impossible possible, make the impossible possible in my life, in the name of Jesus

13. I shall not give up on my good dreams, in the name of Jesus

14. I shall not lose the battle of life to the enemy, in the name of Jesus

DAY 9

Confession: Genesis 42:6
Text: Genesis 31: 10-13; 30: 25-43
Song: Spirit divine attend our prayers
Praise worship: (minimum of 10 minutes)
Prayer of praise and thanksgiving: (minimum of 10 minutes)

PRAYER POINTS

1. I shall arise and shine whether the enemy likes it or not, in the name of Jesus

2. O Lord, let all the God-given potential within me begin to manifest by fire, in the name of Jesus

3. I shall not be relegated to the background, in the name of Jesus

4. My glory shall not be bewitched, in the name of Jesus

5. O Lord, glue me to the riches of the heathen for my inheritance and the uttermost parts of the earth for my possession, in the name of Jesus

6. O Lord, cover me with your glory, in the name of Jesus

7. I shall be fruitful I shall multiply and I shall dominate the earth, in the name of Jesus

8. The promises of God for my life shall be fulfilled whether the enemy likes it or not, in the name of Jesus

9. I shall cooperate with God for the fulfilment of my destiny, in the name of Jesus

10. The star of my destiny shall not die, in the name of Jesus

11. No matter the degree of frustration I shall not shift my focus from Jesus

12. No matter the degree of discouragement I shall not shift my focus from Jesus

13. No matter the degree of deception, I shall not shift my focus from Jesus

14. No matter the degree of intimidation, I shall not shift my focus from Jesus

Day 10

Confession: Genesis 42:6
Text: Genesis 29: 15-30; 2 Kings 5: 1-27
Song: Spirit divine attend our prayers
Praise worship: (minimum of 10 minutes)
Prayer of praise and thanksgiving: (minimum of 10 minutes)

PRAYER POINTS

1. No matter the degree of fear I shall not shift my focus from Jesus
2. I receive the power to see through the lie of the devil concerning my destiny, in the name of Jesus
3. My joy concerning my destiny shall not be short-lived, in the name of Jesus
4. O Lord, give me a wise and discerning heart, in the name of Jesus
5. The blessings of God in my life shall not turn to sorrow, in the name of Jesus
6. I shall not waste God's investment in my life, in the name of Jesus
7. Anything in me that will frustrate God's plans for my life, come out and die, in the name of Jesus
8. The devil shall not write the last chapter of my life, in the name of Jesus
9. I shall not bring disaster on my children and future generation, in the name of Jesus
10. My attitude shall not make God change his mind concerning his blessing in my life, in the name of Jesus

11. O Lord, give me the power to deal with my weaknesses, in the name of Jesus
12. The blessing of God upon my life shall not take me away from the presence of the Lord, in the name of Jesus
13. I shall not bring reproach to the name of the Lord, in the name of Jesus
14. I arrest myself from the path of destruction, in the name of Jesus

SECTION 2

I Shall Fulfil My Divine Destiny

Day 11

Confession: Jeremiah 1:17-19, "*Get yourself ready! Stand up and say to them whatever I command you. Do not be terrified by them, or I will terrify you before them. Today I have made you a fortified city, an iron pillar and a bronze wall to stand against the whole land- against the kings of Judah, its officials, its priests and the people of the land. They will fight against you but will not overcome you, for I am with you and will rescue you," declares the Lord.*"

Text: Jeremiah 1: 17-19

Song: Take my life and let it be

Praise worship: (minimum of 10 minutes)

Prayer of praise and thanksgiving: (minimum of 10 minutes)

PRAYER POINTS

1. O Lord, forgive me my sins and have mercy upon me, in the name of Jesus
2. I close all the doors I have opened for the enemy to attack me, in the name of Jesus
3. I nullify the evil effect of any decision that I took in the past with the blood of Jesus
4. Though I walk through the valley of the shadow of death, I will fear no evil, in the name of Jesus
5. O Lord, give me the grace to rely on you as I obey your instructions concerning my life, in the name of Jesus
6. I refuse to fear because I know that your blessing does not add sorrow, in the name of Jesus

7. Every demonic arrow of fear shot into my life come out and die, in the name of Jesus

8. O Lord save me from enemies that are too strong for me, in the name of Jesus

9. My angel of blessing shall not depart unless he blesses me, in the name of Jesus

10. O Lord, speak solution to all my stubborn problems, in the name of Jesus

11. If you need to change my name to bless me, do it, in the name of Jesus

12. O Lord, energise me to confront my confronter, in the name of Jesus

13. It is my turn for a miracle. I refuse to give up at the edge of success, in the name of Jesus

14. In my struggle with God and with men, I shall overcome, in the name of Jesus

Day 12

Confession: Jeremiah 1:17-19

Text: Esther 3: 7 - 4: 16

Song: Take my life and let it be

Praise worship: (minimum of 10 minutes)

Prayer of praise and thanksgiving: (minimum of 10 minutes)

PRAYER POINTS

1. Every plan of the enemy to destroy my life fail woefully, in the name of Jesus

2. No matter how impossible and desperate my situation is, I shall overcome, in the name of Jesus

3. My enemy do not write me off because my God shall fight for me, in the name of Jesus

4. I am destined to succeed, I refuse to consider failure, in the name of Jesus

5. When the time comes for me to act decisively, fear and anxiety will not paralyse me, in the name of Jesus

6. I am a man on a mission for God, therefore I cannot fail, in the name of Jesus

7. Where others have failed before, I shall succeed, in the name of Jesus

8. I shall not disappoint God when it matters the most, in the name of Jesus

9. The investment of God in my life shall not be wasted, in the name of Jesus

10. O Lord, bless me to be a blessing to others, in the name of Jesus

11. O Lord, the king's heart is in your hand, direct it to favour my cause, in the name of Jesus

12. O Lord, put your words of wisdom and power, that cannot be resisted by any man, into my mouth, in the name of Jesus

13. O Lord, let the irreversible be reversed for my sake today, in the name of Jesus

14. I refuse to put my hand on the plough and look back, in the name of Jesus

Day 13

Confession: Jeremiah 1:17-19
Text: Ruth 1: 1-22 , 4: 1-22
Song: Take my life and let it be
Praise worship: (minimum of 10 minutes)
Prayer of praise and thanksgiving: (minimum of 10 minutes)

PRAYER POINTS

1. O Lord glue my head to my breakthrough, in the name of Jesus
2. Let all things work together for good for me, in the name of Jesus
3. Let every disappointment be converted to divine appointment, in the name of Jesus
4. I move from the land of famine to the land of fruitfulness, in the name of Jesus
5. O Lord, take me from darkness to light, in the name of Jesus
6. I refuse to put my trust in any worthless idol but in God alone, in the name of Jesus
7. O Lord, give me the discernment to recognize you as the only true God and the only one that can help me to reach my goal, in the name of Jesus
8. I am a survivor, not a quitter, in the name of Jesus
9. I have a divine appointment with God and I intend to keep it no power shall stop me, in the name of Jesus
10. I refuse to be discouraged in my divine assignment for God, in the name of Jesus

11. O Lord, give me the grace to exercise the courage and determination that will lead to success in my calling, in the name of Jesus

12. O Lord, let me be at the right place at the right time, in the name of Jesus

13. O Lord, send divine helpers to me from above, in the name of Jesus

14. O Lord, do not replace me with another person, in the name of Jesus

Day 14

Confession: Jeremiah 1:17-19

Text: Acts 9:11-19; Philippians 3:1-14;, Romans 8:28-39; 2 Timothy 4:7-8

Song: Take my life and let it be

Praise worship: (minimum of 10 minutes)

Prayer of praise and thanksgiving: (minimum of 10 minutes)

PRAYER POINTS

1. O thou that hearest prayer, hear my prayer today, in the name of Jesus
2. Every demonic scale blocking my vision, be removed by fire, in the name of Jesus
3. Lord Jesus, you appeared to Saul on the road to Damascus and you set him on the right course, if I am derailing, put me back on course, in the name of Jesus
4. O Lord, fill me with holy ghost and fire so that I can achieve my divine destiny, in the name of Jesus
5. The devil shall not send me on a "wild goose chase", in the name of Jesus
6. I shall not use the intelligence that God gave to me to fight God, in the name of Jesus
7. O Lord, let me not put my confidence in the flesh but in you, to achieve my divine destiny, in the name of Jesus
8. O Lord, give me the power to give up everything for the love of Christ, in the name of Jesus

9. Nothing shall separate me from the love of God that is In Christ Jesus, in the name of Jesus

10. I shall not give an excuse to God for failure, in the name of Jesus

11. O Lord let me never depart from your presence, make me more than a conqueror, in the name of Jesus

12. I refuse to focus on the past, I shall continue to focus on the future, in the name of Jesus

13. O Lord, make me a soul winner for you, in the name of Jesus

14. O Lord, give me the power to fight the good fight, to finish my course and to keep the faith, in the name of Jesus

DAY 15

Confession: Jeremiah 1:17-19
Text: Exodus 2:1-3:22; Numbers 20:1-13, Deuteronomy 32:48-52
Song: Take my life and let it be
Praise worship: (minimum of 10 minutes)
Prayer of praise and thanksgiving: (minimum of 10 minutes)

PRAYER POINTS

1. O Lord, remove from my life any negative spirit that will make me miss it, in the name of Jesus

2. I refuse to move ahead of God by using head knowledge, in the name of Jesus

3. I refuse to use my physical weaknesses as an excuse for not serving God, in the name of Jesus

4. O Lord, enrol me in your school of patience and endurance, in the name of Jesus

5. O Lord, incubate me in your holy ghost fire, in the name of Jesus

6. O Lord, let me be able to see what you see in me, in the name of Jesus

7. O Lord, remove fear and anger from my life, in the name of Jesus

8. Whatever is in my life that will make me disobey you, O Lord, remove it, in the name of Jesus

9. Lord, help me to die to self and be alive in the spirit, in the name of Jesus

10. Anything in me that will make me lose my physical and spiritual reward, die, in the name of Jesus

11. Any door that I have opened to Satan through which he can destroy my life be closed forever, in the name of Jesus

12. I reject the spirit of "Almost There", in the name of Jesus

13. I shall not just see my promised land from afar, I shall enter into it, in the name of Jesus

14. I shall not work for others to enjoy, in the name of Jesus

Day 16

Confession: Jeremiah 1:17-19
Text: Judges 13: 1-17
Song: Take my life and let it be
Praise worship: (minimum of 10 minutes)
Prayer of praise and thanksgiving: (minimum of 10 minutes)

PRAYER POINTS

1. Let the spirit of God begin to prepare me for the tasks ahead of me, in the name of Jesus

2. O Lord, let me recognize your moves in my life, in the name of Jesus

3. I receive the power to put the enemies of my advancement to flight, in the name of Jesus

4. O Lord, use me to deliver others from bondage, in the name of Jesus,

5. My enemies shall not discover the source of my power, in the name of Jesus

6. I refuse to be shaved by any satanic barber, in the name of Jesus

7. I shall not pray the prayer of defeat and death, in the name of Jesus

8. I refuse to box myself into a corner, in the name of Jesus

9. Let my hand be stronger than the hand of my enemies, in the name of Jesus

10. Every agent of the devil sent to bring me down, fail woefully, in the name of Jesus

11. I refuse to set myself up for destruction, in the name of Jesus
12. O Lord, never let me take you for granted, in the name of Jesus
13. The anointing of God upon my life shall not be wasted, in the name of Jesus
14. I shall not engage in actions that will make the spirit of God in my life depart, in the name of Jesus

DAY 17

Confession: Jeremiah 1:17-19
Text: 1 Samuel 13:14; 16:1-13; 17:1-58; 18:1-30; 2 Samuel 2:1-4; 5:1-5
Song: Take my life and let it be
Praise worship: (minimum of 10 minutes)
Prayer of praise and thanksgiving: (minimum of 10 minutes)

PRAYER POINTS

1. I shall not disappoint the confidence that the Lord has put in me, in the name of Jesus
2. While others are afraid and undecided, O Lord give me the boldness to slay my goliath, in the name of Jesus
3. O Lord, give me the grace to seize every divine opportunity to greatness, in the name of Jesus
4. At all times I shall only listen to the voice of God and not to satanic agents attempting to pull me down, in the name of Jesus
5. Every demonic stumbling block on my way to progress, be crushed to irreparable pieces, in the name of Jesus
6. O Lord, give me the power to fight my way to the top, in the name of Jesus
7. O Lord, give me the power to forgive and forget all past wrongs done to me, in the name of Jesus
8. You the spirit of bitterness, lose your hold over my life, in the name of Jesus

9. O Lord, make me a "man after your own heart", in the name of Jesus

10. At all times let me always seek your counsel before I take a decision, in the name of Jesus

11. The purpose of God for my life shall come to pass whether the enemy likes it or not, in the name of Jesus

12. I refuse to surrender to my enemies they must surrender to me, in the name of Jesus

13. I will not be my own worst enemy, I will not use my own hands to slow myself down, in the name of Jesus

14. The devil shall not find work for my idle hands, in the name of Jesus

Day 18

Confession: Jeremiah 1:17-19

Text: Joshua 1:1-18; 21:43-45; 23:14-16

Song: Take my life and let it be

Praise worship: (minimum of 10 minutes)

Prayer of praise and thanksgiving: (minimum of 10 minutes)

PRAYER POINTS

1. I shall possess every place that the soles of my feet shall tread upon, in the name of Jesus
2. O Lord, make me a force to reckon with, all the days of my life, in the name of Jesus
3. I receive the power to arise and pursue God's plans for my life, in the name of Jesus
4. In all that I do, O Lord, never let me depart from your presence, in the name of Jesus
5. The anointing to feast on the word of God day and night, fall upon my life now, in the name of Jesus
6. O Lord make my way prosperous and give me good success, in the name of Jesus
7. O Lord, give unto me the strength and courage that I need to achieve my divine destiny, in the name of Jesus
8. The fear of failure shall not rob me of the joy of fulfilling my divine destiny, in the name of Jesus
9. O Lord, you know the end from the beginning, wake up my fighting spirit, in the name of Jesus

10. Lord Jesus, let me have implicit trust in you to make me successful in life, in the name of Jesus

11. Lord God Almighty, do not fail me, do not forsake me, in the name of Jesus

12. All the promises of God for my life shall come to pass whether the enemy likes it or not, in the name of Jesus

13. O Lord make all the enemies of my advancement bow before me in surrender, in the name of Jesus

14. After the Lord has blessed me, I shall not serve other gods and forget God thereby incurring his wrath, in the name of Jesus

DAY 19

Confession: Jeremiah 1:17-19
Text: 1 kings 3:1-28, 4:29-34; 10:23-26; 11:1-13
Song: Take my life and let it be
Praise worship: (minimum of 10 minutes)
Prayer of praise and thanksgiving: (minimum of 10 minutes)

PRAYER POINTS

1. In my prayer to you O Lord, let me not ask amiss, in the name of Jesus
2. All that I have belongs to you Lord, use them for your glory, in the name of Jesus
3. Lord, you have been so wonderful to me, have your way in my life, in the name of Jesus
4. At all times Lord, let me always humble myself in your presence, in the name of Jesus
5. O Lord give me a wise and understanding heart, in the name of Jesus
6. I refuse to allow the pleasures of this world to take me away from the presence of God, in the name of Jesus
7. I refuse to set myself up for self-destruction, in the name of Jesus
8. Any destiny demoting spirit in my life, die, in the name of Jesus
9. The blessings of God in my life shall not make me stumble, in the name of Jesus
10. The blessing of God in my life shall promote me and not destroy me, in the name of Jesus

11. O Lord, give me the power to love what you love and have what you have, in the name of Jesus

12. I shall not bring a curse upon my children and generation yet unborn by disobeying God, in the name of Jesus

13. O Lord, do not rebuke me in your anger or discipline me in your wrath, in the name of Jesus

14. O Lord, create in me the fear of you and let me avoid all extremes, in the name of Jesus

Day 20

Confession: Jeremiah 1:17-19
Text: Job 1:1-2:13; 42:1-16
Song: Take my life and let it be
Praise worship: (minimum of 10 minutes)
Prayer of praise and thanksgiving: (minimum of 10 minutes)

PRAYER POINTS

1. Every demonic interest in my goodness, cease in the name of Jesus

2. The Lord shall take delight in my goodness, in the name of Jesus

3. The Lord shall be able to boast about my life, in the name of Jesus

4. O Lord, let me learn to worship you always because you are God and not just because you have blessed me, in the name of Jesus

5. The Lord shall not regret that he created me, in the name of Jesus

6. No matter what anybody says, I shall never curse God, in the name of Jesus

7. Holiness and righteousness shall continue to form the bedrock of my relationship with God and man, in the name of Jesus

8. Though I might not understand why certain things happen to me, O Lord, let me continue to trust you with my life, in the name of Jesus

9. O Lord that blessed the latter end of Job more than his beginning, bless my latter years too, in the name of Jesus

10. O Lord, remove the fear of the unknown from my life, in the name of Jesus

11. People shall praise God because of my life, in the name of Jesus
12. The will of God for my life shall come to pass, whether the enemy likes it or not, in the name of Jesus
13. I shall fulfil my divine destiny, whether the enemy likes it or not, in the name of Jesus
14. Thank the Lord for answered prayers.

SECTION 3

Owners Of Evil Load Carry Your Load

Day 21

Confession: Esther 7:9-10, "*Then Harbona, one of the eunuchs attending the king, said "a gallows seventy-five feet high stands by Haman's house. He had it made for Mordecai, who spoke up to help the king." The king said, "Hang him on it!" So they hanged Haman on the gallows he had prepared for Mordecai. Then the king's fury subsided.*

Text: Esther 7: 1-8

Song: Rock of Ages cleft for me

Praise worship: (minimum of 10 minutes)

Prayer of praise and thanksgiving: (minimum of 10 minutes)

PRAYER POINTS

1. The evil plan of the enemy concerning my life shall not stand, in the name of Jesus
2. The authority given to the enemy to destroy me shall work against my enemy, in the name of Jesus
3. I shall not die before my time, in the name of Jesus
4. The purpose for which God created me shall be achieved whether the enemy likes it or not, in the name of Jesus
5. The rage of the enemy concerning my life shall backfire on the enemy, in the name of Jesus
6. My God that I serve shall not abandon me to the teeth of the wicked, in the name of Jesus
7. The victory of the enemy over my life shall be short-lived, in the name of Jesus

8. O Lord, open your "book of remembrance" and promote me, in the name of Jesus

9. Let my enemy become my stepping stone to my greatness, in the name of Jesus

10. I refuse to bow down to the enemy, my enemy shall bow down before me, in the name of Jesus

11. Owners of evil load, carry your load with both hands, in the name of Jesus

12. My Haman shall die in my place, in the name of Jesus

13. My Haman shall be hung in the gallows that he has prepared for me, in the name of Jesus

14. Let the carefully prepared plan of my enemy to destroy me, blow up in his face, in the name of Jesus

DAY 22

Confession: Esther 6: 13
Text: Micah 7: 5-7
Song: Rock of Ages cleft for me
Praise worship: (minimum of 10 minutes)
Prayer of praise and thanksgiving: (minimum of 10 minutes)

PRAYER POINTS

1. I refuse to put my trust in man rather I shall trust in God at all times, in the name of Jesus

2. I will not supply my enemy with the information to destroy me, in the name of Jesus

3. O Lord, protect me from all unfriendly friends, in the name of Jesus

4. My calling and ministry shall not be bewitched, in the name of Jesus

5. O Lord, expose and disgrace every household enemy manipulating my life for evil, in the name of Jesus

6. O Lord make me too hot for the enemy to handle, in the name of Jesus

7. Let the enemy who changed himself into a serpent to harm me, die the death of a serpent, in the name of Jesus

8. O Lord, turn every evil sleep of the enemy engaged upon to harm me into a dead sleep, in the name of Jesus

9. I wash off every witchcraft mark placed upon my life, with the blood of Jesus

10. Every envious friend and relation setting me up for destruction, die, in the name of Jesus

11. Let my life be resistant to every satanic insult, in the name of Jesus

12. O Lord, begin to terrorize every enemy of my advancement, in the name of Jesus

13. Let every unrepentant adversary be clothed with shame and reproach, in the name of Jesus

14. Let every unrepentant adversary collapse and die, in the name of Jesus

Day 23

Confession: Esther 6: 13
Text: 1 Samuel 24: 1-22
Song: Rock of Ages cleft for me
Praise worship: (minimum of 10 minutes)
Prayer of praise and thanksgiving: (minimum of 10 minutes)

PRAYER POINTS

1. O Lord deliver my enemies into my hands today, in the name of Jesus

2. O Lord cause my enemies to make mistakes that will put them at my mercy, in the name of Jesus

3. O Lord restrain me from taking revenge on my enemies myself, in the name of Jesus

4. O Lord, judge between me and my enemies and avenge me of them, in the name of Jesus

5. O Lord, frustrate the efforts of the enemy seeking my life, in the name of Jesus

6. O Lord, deliver me from the hand of my enemies, in the name of Jesus

7. O Lord, thoroughly disgrace every unrepentant power seeking to take my life, in the name of Jesus

8. The harder the enemy tries to destroy me the harder he shall fall, in the name of Jesus

9. Let my enemy start his day in confusion and end it in destruction, in the name of Jesus

10. Let my enemy be forced to recognize your hand of protection over my life, in the name of Jesus

11. Let my enemy see your glory in my life and begin to fear you, in the name of Jesus

12. Let God arise and let all my enemies scatter, in the name of Jesus

13. O Lord arise in your anger and fight my battles for me, in the name of Jesus

14. No weapon fashioned against me shall prosper, in the name of Jesus

Day 24

Confession: Esther 6: 13
Text: Psalms 35: 1-28
Song: Rock of Ages cleft for me
Praise worship: (minimum of 10 minutes)
Prayer of praise and thanksgiving: (minimum of 10 minutes)

PRAYER POINTS

1. Contend with those who contend with me, fight against those who fight against me, in the name of Jesus

2. O Lord put every power-seeking after my soul to shame, in the name of Jesus

3. Let every enemy of my advancement begin to run without a pursuer, in the name of Jesus

4. O Lord, give my enemies no rest, in the name of Jesus

5. Let the evil of the wicked slay them, in the name of Jesus

6. O Lord, declare my enemies guilty and Let their intrigues be their downfall, in the name of Jesus

7. O Lord, make the path of my enemies dark and slippery and let the angel of the Lord persecute them, in the name of Jesus

8. Let destruction come upon my enemies unawares, in the name of Jesus

9. Let the net that he had hidden for me, catch him, in the name of Jesus

10. Let my enemy use his own hands to destroy himself, in the name of Jesus

11. Instead of the evil, the enemy has planned for me I shall rejoice in the Lord, in the name of Jesus

12. O Lord, let not my enemy rejoice over my life, in the name of Jesus

13. O Lord, cloth my enemies with shame and dishonour, in the name of Jesus

14. Let all my enemies turn back in sudden disgrace, in the name of Jesus

Day 25

Confession: Esther 6: 13
Text: Psalms 109: 1-31
Song: Rock of Ages cleft for me
Praise worship: (minimum of 10 minutes)
Prayer of praise and thanksgiving: (minimum of 10 minutes)

PRAYER POINTS

1. O Lord, do not remain silent concerning my situation, in the name of Jesus

2. I condemn all lying tongues rising in judgement against me, in the name of Jesus

3. I come against every unfriendly friend who has decided to repay me evil for good and hatred for my friendship, by fire, in the name of Jesus

4. When my enemies are tried let them be found guilty, in the name of Jesus

5. Let the prayer of the enemies of my advancement condemn them, in the name of Jesus

6. May the days of the enemy of my advancement be few, in the name of Jesus

7. May no one extend kindness to the enemies of my advancement, in the name of Jesus

8. May the sins of my enemies always remain before the Lord, in the name of Jesus

9. Let the curses pronounced on me by my enemies come upon them, in the name of Jesus

10. Since my unrepentant enemies found no pleasure in blessing may blessing be far from them, in the name of Jesus

11. Let every evil that my enemies have been wishing me begin to manifest in their life's, in the name of Jesus

12. O Lord, convert every curse of the enemy against my life to blessings for me, in the name of Jesus

13. O Lord, give me aid against my enemies for the help of man is worthless, in the name of Jesus

14. O Lord, save me from bloodthirsty men, in the name of Jesus

Day 26

Confession: Esther 6: 13
Text: Matthew 13: 24-30
Song: Rock of Ages cleft for me
Praise worship: (minimum of 10 minutes)
Prayer of praise and thanksgiving: (minimum of 10 minutes)

PRAYER POINTS

1. Every enemy sowing weed among the wheat of my life die, in the name of Jesus

2. I refuse to be spiritually asleep, in the name of Jesus

3. O Lord, let me be spiritually alert at all times, in the name of Jesus

4. Every evil planted into my life by the enemy, be roasted by fire, in the name of Jesus,

5. My life, begin to reject all evil seeds in the name of Jesus

6. My life shall not be a fertile ground for evil to thrive, in the name of Jesus

7. O Lord, let me cooperate with you as you try to remove weeds from the wheat of my life, in the name of Jesus

8. Every tree that the Lord has not planted in my life be uprooted by fire, in the name of Jesus

9. I refused to be a willing tool in the hand of the enemy, in the name of Jesus

10. O Lord, let my life be allergic to sin, in the name of Jesus

11. Let the angels of God begin to plant good seeds into my life, in the name of Jesus

12. Every power planning to plant evil seed into my life, stumble and fall, in the name of Jesus

13. Let the enemies begin to weep uncontrollable and be in constant sorrow, in the name of Jesus

14. Every evil bird flying for my sake somersault and die, in the name of Jesus

DAY 27

Confession: Esther 6: 13
Text: 1 Samuel 5:1-12; Job 5:12-16; Proverbs 26:2
Song: Rock of Ages cleft for me
Praise worship: (minimum of 10 minutes)
Prayer of praise and thanksgiving: (minimum of 10 minutes)

PRAYER POINTS

1. Let my picture on any evil altar catch fire, in the name of Jesus
2. O Lord, let all the diviners speaking evil concerning my life, go mad, in the name of Jesus
3. Just as Balaam could not curse the Israelites, no evil priest shall be able to curse me, in the name of Jesus
4. When my name is called at any evil altar, Lord Jesus appear to them, in the name of Jesus
5. I reject any evil summon, in the name of Jesus
6. Let the power backing any evil priest in charge of my case rise and destroy him, in the name of Jesus
7. O Lord, let "your hand be sore" upon the evil priests and the powers that they depend on, in the name of Jesus
8. Let your terror fall upon all evil priests in charge of my case, in the name of Jesus
9. O Lord, afflict all evil priests divining against me with tumours, in the name of Jesus
10. Let commotion break out in the shrine of the evil priest concerning my case, in the name of Jesus

11. O Lord, if my enemies refuse to hands off my matter let their obituary be announced, in the name of Jesus

12. I retrieve all my virtues stolen by evil priests and placed on any evil altar by fire, in the name of Jesus

13. I retrieve any organ of my body placed on any evil altar by fire, in the name of Jesus

14. Let my virtues become too hot in the hands of evil priests and let them begin to seek ways to return them to me, in the name of Jesus

DAY 28

Confession: Esther 6: 13
Text: 2 Samuel 15: 1-37
Song: Rock of Ages cleft for me
Praise worship: (minimum of 10 minutes)
Prayer of praise and thanksgiving: (minimum of 10 minutes)

PRAYER POINTS

1. Every plot of the enemy to displace me, fail woefully, in the name of Jesus

2. Every power double-crossing my blessings, be exposed and disgraced, in the name of Jesus

3. Every spirit of manipulation, turning people's hearts against me, be destroyed by fire, in the name of Jesus

4. O Lord, do not hide from me the evil being planned by the enemy against me, in the name of Jesus

5. O Lord, confuse the tongues of evil men gathered against me, in the name of Jesus

6. Let the victory of the enemy over my life be temporary and short-lived, in the name of Jesus

7. I refuse to panic even in the face of all the problems I am going through, in the name of Jesus

8. O Lord, give me the peace of mind and the courage to make the right decisions during my moments of crisis, in the name of Jesus

9. O Lord, turn the counsel of every Ahithophel working for my enemies into foolishness, in the name of Jesus

10. Let my seat become too hot for the enemy to sit upon, in the name of Jesus

11. Let there be confusion, chaos and death in the camp of the enemies of my advancements, in the name of Jesus

12. O Lord, see how my enemies persecute me. Have mercy and lift me from the gates of death, in the name of Jesus

13. O Lord turn my wailing into dancing, remove my sackcloth and clothe me with joy, in the name of Jesus

14. O Lord, put the right words into my mouth to defeat the enemies of my advancement, in the name of Jesus

Day 29

Confession: Esther 6: 13
Text: Psalms 92: 1-15
Song: Rock of Ages cleft for me
Praise worship: (minimum of 10 minutes)
Prayer of praise and thanksgiving: (minimum of 10 minutes)

PRAYER POINTS

1. Every prayer resisting demon, be roasted by fire, in the name of Jesus

2. I command blindness on all evil monitoring eyes, in the name of Jesus

3. All evil powers seeking reinforcement against me, be frustrated, in the name of Jesus

4. Every power trying to waste my divine destiny, be wasted, in the name of Jesus

5. Every demonic harvester that has harvested my blessing, release it by fire, in the name of Jesus

6. Every evil spiritual twin confiscating my blessing receive the thunder fire of God and die, in the name of Jesus

7. Every demonic ladder, through which the enemy climbed into my life, be roasted by fire, in the name of Jesus

8. Every power trying to turn my life upside down, loose your hold over my life, in the name of Jesus

9. You ground, hear the word of the Lord and bring forth all my virtues kept inside you by evil powers, in the name of Jesus

10. Let my life begin to confuse every observer in the name of Jesus

11. O Lord, exalt my horn like that of a unicorn and pour fresh oil upon me, in the name of Jesus

12. My eyes shall see the defeat of my adversaries and my ears shall hear the rout of my wicked foes, in the name of Jesus

13. I boldly declare that no evil power shall be able to touch me and neither can they do me any harm, in the name of Jesus

14. Thank the Lord for freeing you from your chains.

DAY 30

Confession: Esther 6: 13
Text: Daniel 6: 1- 28
Song: Rock of Ages cleft for me
Praise worship: (minimum of 10 minutes)
Prayer of praise and thanksgiving: (minimum of 10 minutes)

PRAYER POINTS

1. You the spirit of envy and jealously loose your hold over my life in the name of Jesus

2. Let the power to live a holy life, fall upon my life, in the name of Jesus

3. My life shall not bring reproach to God, in the name of Jesus

4. Every evil agreement by my enemies against my advancement, backfire, in the name of Jesus

5. I refused to be intimidated by the enemies of my advancement, in the name of Jesus

6. Nothing shall stop me from serving my God, even the threat of death, in the name of Jesus

7. O God, make kings and princes lose their sleep, over my situation, in the name of Jesus

8. My God whom I serve continually shall rescue me from all physical and spiritual lions, in the name of Jesus

9. O Lord, send your angel to shut the mouths of lions sent to destroy me, in the name of Jesus

10. Let all those who falsely accuse me be devoured by spiritual and physical lions, in the name of Jesus

11. On account of me, people shall serve the Lord, in the name of Jesus

12. I shall make a difference in my generation, in the name of Jesus

13. Thou God that rescued Daniel from the attack of lions rescue me from the attacks of my enemies, in the name of Jesus

14. O Lord, prosper me as you prospered Daniel in the land of Babylon, in the name of Jesus.

SECTION 4

I Move Forward By Fire

DAY 31

Confession: Mark 10:51-52, "*What do you want me to do for you?" Jesus asked him. The blind man said, "Rabbi, I want to see". "Go, "Jesus said, "your faith has healed you." Immediately he received his sight and followed Jesus along the road.*

Text: Mark 10: 46- 50

Song: Thine forever God of love

Praise worship: (minimum of 10 minutes)

Prayer of praise and thanksgiving: (minimum of 10 minutes)

PRAYER POINTS

1. I shall not miss my divine opportunity for blessing, in the name of Jesus
2. O Lord give me the power to seize every divine opportunity that you send to me, in the name of Jesus
3. I shall not keep silent when I am expected to cry to you for help, in the name of Jesus
4. No demon in hell can stop me from receiving my miracles from you, in the name of Jesus
5. Nothing and absolutely nothing shall make me shift my focus from Jesus, in the name of Jesus
6. I command the voice of the enemy to be silenced concerning my life, in the name of Jesus
7. Let my prayers attract divine attention and sponsor divine action, in the name of Jesus

8. As I call on the Lord, he will hear me and save me from all my troubles, in the name of Jesus

9. Let the power of the wicked over my life be broken, in the name of Jesus

10. O Lord, help me and deliver me from the wicked because I take refuge in you, in the name of Jesus

11. O Lord let every demonic stumbling block become my stepping stone to greatness, in the name of Jesus

12. Every garment of poverty be roasted by fire, in the name of Jesus

13. Every garment of shame and reproach, be roasted by fire, in the name of Jesus

14. Lord Jesus let your healing power fall upon every situation in my life that does not glorify God, in the name of Jesus

Day 32

Confession: Mark 10:51-52
Text: Exodus 14: 10-31
Song: Thine forever God of love
Praise worship: (minimum of 10 minutes)
Prayer of praise and thanksgiving: (minimum of 10 minutes)

PRAYER POINTS

1. My God is greater than any problems that I have, in the name of Jesus

2. Every power prolonging my stay in Egypt, fall down and die, in the name of Jesus

3. Every spirit of fear and anxiety operating in my life come out and die, in the name of Jesus

4. The Egyptians that I see now I shall see them no more, in the name of Jesus

5. O Lord make a way for me where there is no way, in the name of Jesus

6. Every red sea situation in my life, be parted, in the name of Jesus

7. Every stubborn pursuer of my destiny die, in the name of Jesus

8. O Lord look down from heaven and judge the enemies of my advancement, in the name of Jesus

9. O Lord let all the enemies of my destiny experience you as the mighty terrible one, with the blood of Jesus

10. Let the joy of the enemies of my destiny be suddenly turned to sorrow, in the name of Jesus

11. I shall have the last laugh over my enemies, in the name of Jesus

12. O Lord, set a trap for my enemies and let them be caught in their craftiness, in the name of Jesus

13. O Lord fight for me today against the enemies of my advancement, in the name of Jesus

14. I reject the spirit of backwardness. I move forward by fire, in the name of Jesus

DAY 33

Confession: Mark 10: 51-52
Text: 2 Kings 7: 1-20
Song: Thine forever God of love
Praise worship: (minimum of 10 minutes)
Prayer of praise and thanksgiving: (minimum of 10 minutes)

PRAYER POINTS

1. O Lord you are the God of impossibilities make the impossible possible in my life, in the name of Jesus
2. O Lord, you are not a man that you will lie, let all your promises for my life come to pass, in the name of Jesus
3. O Lord, give me the faith that moves mountains, in the name of Jesus
4. O Lord, reverse the irreversible in my life, in the name of Jesus
5. O Lord, move me from the position of not enough to that of more than enough, in the name of Jesus
6. Every power, speaking impossibility into my situation die, in the name of Jesus
7. I come against every spirit of doubt in my life, in the name of Jesus
8. O Lord, cause my enemies to hear terrifying noises, in the name of Jesus
9. I send confusion into the camp of the enemies of my advancement, in the name of Jesus

10. Let my enemy begin to run without a pursuer, in the name of Jesus

11. O Lord make a divine provision for me for my advancement, in the name of Jesus

12. I reject and cancel with the blood of Jesus all negative words spoken against my advancement, in the name of Jesus

13. I plunder the camp of the wicked today, in the name of Jesus

14. My time of rejoicing has come my period of lack and want is over, in the name of Jesus

Day 34

Confession: Mark 10:51-52
Text: 1 Kings 18: 16-46
Song: Thine forever God of love
Praise worship: (minimum of 10 minutes)
Prayer of praise and thanksgiving: (minimum of 10 minutes)

PRAYER POINTS

1. O Lord begin to trouble every troubler of the Israel of my destiny, in the name of Jesus

2. My problems shall receive a solution today, in the name of Jesus

3. Any satanic priest ministering at any evil altar against my advancement, die, in the name of Jesus

4. I mock the prophets of Baal working against my destiny today, in the name of Jesus

5. O Lord let it be known that you are God in my life, in the name of Jesus

6. The powers that my enemies depend upon shall fail them, in the name of Jesus

7. O Lord, frustrate the efforts of the pursuer of my destiny, in the name of Jesus

8. When I call upon you O Lord, answer my prayers by fire, in the name of Jesus

9. Anything in my life resisting the move of the holy spirit is destroyed by fire, in the name of Jesus

10. O Lord, repair all that is needed to be repaired for me to be useful to you, in the name of Jesus

11. O Lord cause the rain of abundance to fall upon my life, in the name of Jesus

12. O Lord, manifest yourself as the almighty in my situation, in the name of Jesus

13. O Lord, completely destroy the wicked powers attacking my destiny, in the name of Jesus

14. I receive the power to confront my confronter. I move from the valley to the mountain top, in the name of Jesus

DAY 35

Confession: Mark 10:51-52
Text: Daniel 3: 1-30
Song: Thine forever God of love
Praise worship: (minimum of 10 minutes)
Prayer of praise and thanksgiving: (minimum of 10 minutes)

PRAYER POINTS

1. At all times I shall put my focus on God and not on man, in the name of Jesus

2. O God in you I put my trust, do not let me be put to shame, in the name of Jesus

3. Every power or satanic agents broadcasting my name for evil purposes, die, in the name of Jesus

4. You that power, stirring resentment against my advancement perish by fire, in the name of Jesus

5. I refuse to fear man and disobey God, in the name of Jesus

6. O Lord my life is in your hands save me from the range of my enemies, in the name of Jesus

7. O Lord, hear my cries and deliver me from all my troubles, in the name of Jesus

8. I will never worship "man-made god", in the name of Jesus

9. Every human agent sent on errand against my life be roasted by fire, in the name of Jesus

10. Every demonic fire prepared by the enemy to terminate my life be powerless over me, in the name of Jesus

11. Lord Jesus be the fourth man in the fire with me after the order of Shadrach, Meshach and Abednego, in the name of Jesus

12. Let my life become a living testimony, in the name of Jesus

13. O Lord turn the heart of the enemy into an air-conditioner for me, in the name of Jesus

14. O Lord use what the enemy intends to use to bring me down, to promote me, in the name of Jesus

DAY 36

Confession: Mark 10:51-52
Text: Micah 7:8
Song: Thine forever God of love
Praise worship: (minimum of 10 minutes)
Prayer of praise and thanksgiving: (minimum of 10 minutes)

PRAYER POINTS

1. My enemy, do not gloat over me through I have fallen I will rise again, in the name of Jesus

2. Anything in me inviting failure into my life dies, in the name of Jesus

3. I refuse to stay in the valley of failure I climb the mountain of success, in the name of Jesus

4. I shall not take the back position in life, in the name of Jesus,

5. I shall not carry shoes for my mates, in the name of Jesus

6. I Reject the spirit of poverty and lack, in the name of Jesus

7. I refuse to cooperate with the enemy to destroy my destiny, in the name of Jesus

8. You the spirit of profitless hard work, I paralyse you today, in the name of Jesus

9. O Lord refresh me as I refresh others, in the name of Jesus

10. Every demonic stumbling block on my way of advancement be slashed unto desolation, in the name of Jesus

11. Every failure mechanism programmed into my life malfunction, in the name of Jesus

12. Every remote power controlling me to fail somersault and die, in the name of Jesus

13. My life, come out of the prison of failure, in the name of Jesus

14. Whether the enemy likes it or not my promotion shall be announced, in the name of Jesus

Day 37

Confession: Mark 10:51-52
Text: 1 Chronicles 4: 9-10
Song: Thine forever God of love
Praise worship: (minimum of 10 minutes)
Prayer of praise and thanksgiving: (minimum of 10 minutes)

PRAYER POINTS

1. I reject every evil name, in the name of Jesus

2. I refuse to live with the mistakes of my parents, in the name of Jesus

3. My promotion shall not be dependent on the tongues of men, in the name of Jesus

4. I refuse to give an excuse to the Lord for living a life of failure, in the name of Jesus

5. Let the evil effect of any negative name be powerless over me, in the name of Jesus

6. (sing this song) Don't allow me, don't allow me, don't allow me, Jesus, to go empty-handed

7. O Lord position me for blessing in this programme, in the name of Jesus

8. O Lord bless me indeed, in the name of Jesus

9. O Lord, enlarge my coast, in the name of Jesus

10. Let the anointing of increase fall upon the works of my hands, in the name of Jesus

11. O Lord let your hands be with me, in the name of Jesus
12. O Lord keep me from harm so that I will be free from pain, in the name of Jesus
13. O Lord let your word be a lamp to my feet and a light for my path, in the name of Jesus
14. O Lord answer my prayers as you answered Jabez, in the name of Jesus

Day 38

Confession: Mark 10:51-52
Text: 2 Kings 4: 1-7
Song: Thine forever God of love
Praise worship: (minimum of 10 minutes)
Prayer of praise and thanksgiving: (minimum of 10 minutes)

PRAYER POINTS

1. Every garment of poverty, be roasted by fire, in the name of Jesus

2. Every garment of shame and reproach, be roasted by fire, in the name of Jesus

3. The plans of the enemy shall not come to pass in my life, in the name of Jesus

4. O Lord, do not allow my enemies to ask me for the evidence of the God that I serve, in the name of Jesus

5. O Lord, establish me as I believe in you and prosper me as I believe your prophets, in the name of Jesus

6. O Lord, help me to identify the seed of greatness that you have planted into my life, in the name of Jesus

7. Let me follow your prescription for greatness without any doubt, in the name of Jesus

8. I shall not limit God with my head knowledge, in the name of Jesus

9. I shall obey God fully and not partially, in the name of Jesus

10. Those who have written me off will have no choice than to reckon with me, in the name of Jesus

11. O Lord, supply all my needs according to your riches in glory by Christ Jesus

12. I shall not live a life of struggle and regret, in the name of Jesus

13. O Lord provide for me all that I require to live a life of comfort all the days of my life, in the name of Jesus

14. Let my divine insurance begin to yield dividends now, in the name of Jesus

Day 39

Confession: Mark 10:51-52
Text: Acts 8: 26-38
Song: Thine forever God of love
Praise worship: (minimum of 10 minutes)
Prayer of praise and thanksgiving: (minimum of 10 minutes)\

PRAYER POINTS

1. O Lord send divine helpers to move me forward by fire, in the name of Jesus

2. O Lord, promote me physically and spiritually, in the name of Jesus

3. Let me recognize your hand in my life, in the name of Jesus

4. I shall not scare away my divine helpers, in the name of Jesus

5. O Lord take a personal interest in my spiritual development, in the name of Jesus

6. The spirit of "too know" shall not destroy my life, in the name of Jesus

7. Let me recognize my spiritual limitation and continually hunger for you, in the name of Jesus

8. O Lord, give me a gentle and humble spirit that is willing to learn at your feet, in the name of Jesus

9. O Lord, bless me to be a blessing to others, in the name of Jesus

10. O Lord make me an instrument worthy of your use, in the name of Jesus

11. Let me fit into your "big picture" for my generation, in the name of Jesus

12. O Lord prepare me for the big task of evangelism in front of me, in the name of Jesus

13. The blessing that God has given to me shall not stand in my way of doing God's work, in the name of Jesus

14. My life shall not disappoint God rather I shall be a useful tool in the house of God, in the name of Jesus.

DAY 40

Confession: Mark 10:51-52
Text: Matthew 25: 1-30
Song: Thine forever God of love
Praise worship: (minimum of 10 minutes)
Prayer of praise and thanksgiving: (minimum of 10 minutes)

PRAYER POINTS

1. Let the anointing to take wise and intelligent decisions fall upon my life, in the name of Jesus

2. O Lord give me the power to always consider the spiritual implications of my decisions, in the name of Jesus

3. I shall not lose out in the race of life, in the name of Jesus

4. I reject every spirit of failure at the edge of a breakthrough, in the name of Jesus

5. O Lord, make me ready for you at all times, in the name of Jesus

6. My position in heaven shall not be vacant, in the name of Jesus

7. The door of success shall not be shut against me, in the name of Jesus

8. I shall not betray the confidence that God has in me, in the name of Jesus

9. Though I start small, I shall not remain small, in the name of Jesus

10. I shall not bury the talent that God has given to me, in the name of Jesus

11. I shall not be a benchwarmer in the house of God, in the name of Jesus

12. The gifts that God has given to me shall not be withdrawn and given to other people, in the name of Jesus

13. I command every rebellious and judgmental spirit in my life to die, in the name of Jesus

14. I shall not use the clock of other people's lives to run my own life, in the name of Jesus.

ABOUT AUTHOR

Pastor Seyi Ogunorunyinka, a minister of the Gospel, is anointed and gifted in healing and deliverance, spiritual warfare and in the power of the Holy Spirit. A prophet called by GOD and being used to release empowerment for abundance and victory in the lives of believers. Through his ministry, lives are being touched daily with the power of the Holy Spirit leading to peace and restoration to GOD's abundant life.

Pastor Seyi Ogunorunyinka is the Pastor of the Promised Land Restoration Ministries (PLRM) based in Lagos, Nigeria. PLRM is a ministry standing on the truth of GOD'S word and whose vision is propelled by the Holiness and Righteousness of GOD.

www.ingramcontent.com/pod-product-compliance
Lightning Source LLC
LaVergne TN
LVHW010452160826
845677LV00012B/2449
9798417889479